The Migraine Hotel

LUKE KENNARD is a poet, critic, dramatist and pugilist. He is compassionate, but prone to anxiety and bleak introspection. Many have called him polite and quite funny, but add that he suffers from a tendency towards constant nervous laughter and an apparently involuntary rictus of disdain. His poetry and criticism have appeared in *Stride Magazine, Sentence, Echo:Location, The Tall Lighthouse Review, Reactions 4, Orbis, 14 Magazine, The Flying Post, Exultations & Difficulties*. He won an Eric Gregory Award in 2005 and was shortlisted for Best Collection in the 2007 Forward Poetry Prizes. He is quite tall.

Also by Luke Kennard

The Solex Brothers and Other Poems (Redux) (Salt)
The Harbour Beyond the Movie (Salt)

The Migraine Hotel

Luke Kennard

SALT

CAMBRIDGE

PUBLISHED BY SALT PUBLISHING
14a High Street, Fulbourn, Cambridge CB21 5DH United Kingdom

© Luke Kennard 2009

The right of Luke Kennard to be identified as the
author of this work has been asserted by him in accordance
with Section 77 of the Copyright, Designs and Patents Act 1988.

Salt Publishing 2009
Reprinted 2009

Printed in Great Britain by the MPG Books Group, Bodmin and King's Lynn

Typeset in Swift 9.5 / 13

ISBN 978 1 84471 555 8 paperback

Salt Publishing Ltd gratefully acknowledges
the financial assistance of Arts Council England

1 3 5 7 9 8 6 4 2

To Andy Brown
For patience and insight — the only real benefaction

Contents

Acknowledgements

'Wolf on the Couch' in *Mimesis*. 'A Dog Descends', 'A Sure Fire Sign', 'Pleasure Beach', 'My Friend', 'Addiction Clinic' and 'Four Neighbours' in *Succour Magazine*. 'The Dusty Era' and 'Variations on Tears' in *The Manhattan Review*. 'Sexual Fantasies of the Inuit Warriors' in *With*. A version of 'A Terrorist, Maybe, With his Children' in *Fuselit*. 'Grapefruit' and 'Gravedigger: The Movie' in *Bat City Review*. 'Painful Revisions' in *Rising*. 'Five Poems for a New Shopping Centre' in *The Tall Lighthouse Review*. 'Repetition' in Shadow Train, 'Bestiary for the Seven Days' in *Dusie*, 'The Last Days of Advertising' in *The London Magazine*. 'And I Saw' and 'Estate' in *Tears in the Fence*. 'The Six Times My Heart Broke' in *Pomegranate*. Many thanks to Tim Wells, Jon Stone, James Midgely, Todd Swift, Phil Fried, Anthony Banks, Rupert Loydell, Charlotte Geater, Les Robinson, Jeffrey Side, Ian Seed and David Caddy.

Grateful acknowledgement is due to the AHRC for providing the resources and funding to write these and other works at the Centre for Creative Writing and Arts, University of Exeter and the University of Birmingham to whom also is due thanks for the space, both mental and physical, to write.

Heartfelt thanks to Zoë Kennard for putting up with me saying 'I'm rubbish. It's rubbish, isn't it? I hate everything I've ever written.' every five minutes.

My Friend

My friend, your irresponsibility and your unhappiness delight me. Your financial problems and your expanding waist-line are a constant source of relief. I am so happy you drink more than I do and that you don't seem to enjoy it as much. When I hear you being arrogant and argumentative, my heart leaps. Your nihilism is fast becoming the richest source of meaning in my life and it is my pleasure to watch you speaking harshly to others. When you gossip about our mutual acquaintances I sigh with satisfaction. Your childish impatience delights me. The day you threw a tantrum in the middle of the supermarket was the happiest day of my life. Sometimes you say something which reveals you to be rather stupid—and I love you then, but not as much as I love you when you are callously manipulative. Your promiscuity is like a faithful dog at my side. When you talk about your petty affairs, you try to make them sound grand and important—I cherish your gaucheness and your flippancy. At times it seems your are actually without a sense of humour: I bless the day I met you. You bully people younger and weaker than you—and when others tell me about this, I am pleased. Sometimes I think you are incapable of love—and I am filled with the contentment of waking on a Saturday morning to realise I don't have to go to work. I often suspect that you do not even *like* me and my laughter overflows like water from a blocked cistern.

The Dusty Era
for S.F.

One day he was walking behind her with several colleagues from the Embassy when the hairgrip fell out of her hair (bronze, decorated with three parrots) and clattered to the pavement. It was Stockholm, and high winter. She was deep in conversation with a girlfriend and didn't hear. His colleagues chuckled and continued to admire her legs.

They walked five blocks before she noticed her hair around her shoulders, patted the back of her head and stopped walking. She turned and looked first at the pavement and then up, where she caught his eye. She looked hurt, as if something in his face had apologised for conspiring against her with lesser men (he responded with an apologetic grimace) then she took her girlfriend's arm and walked on, hurriedly.

Two summers later, looking for cufflinks for the reception, he found the hairgrip in a pawn shop in Östersund. An event Grabes describes as, 'One of those overdetermined little moments that gradually conspired to snap his reason like a chicken bone and force him into organised religion, more credulous than even the altar boy.' (*ibid*, p. 136) It should be noted that Grabes was one of the men walking with him that winter evening in 1956, and that he was, in all probability, quite attracted to E. himself—a fact that throws Grabes's more spiteful observations into relief.

He stood with a hip-flask, complaining in the port, a parcel of Christmas presents under one arm. Each day contains a hundred subtle chasms. You can betray someone by not smiling, murder them by not saying 'Mm,' at the appropriate points in the conversation.

Years later he sat on the swingset in the playpark, an unopened letter from his daughter in his inside pocket. He was throwing pine-cones at the rusty ice-cream van. 'You should be banned from describing anyone,' he said out loud in the condensation. Two of his would-be future biographers crashed into each other on the autobahn and were killed instantly. One of them was me, hence my omniscience.

The Embassy was dustier after that—it came to be known as the Age of Dust or the Dusty Era. A fault on the line made the intercom pop sporadically like a man about to say something difficult.

Variations On Tears

I realise you never cry because the last of your tears have been anthologised as a *Collected* and you can't stand the idea of appendices. But what am I to make of the demonstrators playing cards with your daughters? Have they betrayed your estate? Go tell the children to gather their strength for the inevitable backlash.

I realise you never cry because each one of your tears contains a tiny stage on which a gorgeous, life-affirming comedy is always playing and it cheers you up the minute you begin. But what am I to make of the bare interior of your house? You're waiting for inspiration, right? Go tell the children to gather dust on the shelves of archive halls.

I realise you never cry because to do so would be to admit defeat to your harlequin tormentors—wringing their hands at the sides of their eyes and making bleating sounds—and you don't want to give them the satisfaction. But what am I to make of the *Make Your Own Make Your Own* _____ *Kit,* the first instruction of which is 'Have a good idea for something'? Could I have not worked that out for myself? Go tell the children to gather followers for our new religion.

I realise you never cry because you are a total arsehole who cannot even muster enough compassion to feel sorry for *himself.* But what am I to make of your red, blotchy eyes when, as your pharmacist, I know for a fact you are not allergic to anything? Have you, after all, been crying? Go tell the children to gather my remains from the ditch and look out for the white bull who, I'm told, is still at large.

I realise you never cry because the last time you cried four separate murders were reported on the evening news, each one more grisly and inexplicable than the last, and you incorrectly assume there was a correlation. But what am I to make of this terrifying breakfast? Are you trying to get rid of me? Go tell the children to gather the farmers from their taverns to gather the new crop of thorns.

I realise you never cry because when you do, you are beset by birds with long tails and brightly coloured plumage and sharp, hook-like beaks who are uncontrollably drawn towards salt. But what am I to make of your statement, 'The world is not built on metaphors'? What exactly do you think the statement 'The world is not built on metaphors' is? Go tell the children to gather in the clearing and await further instruction.

And I Saw

A false prophet slapped in the face by a wave;
A woman screaming at her clarinet,
'What would you have me do, then, drown you, too?'
Remaindered novels washed up on the shore.
A cat, baffled by a drowsy lobster, jogged
Over the pebbles towing a little carriage.
And the cat didn't say anything—because
It was a cat. And the carriage was not full
Of tiny men, a watermelon or an
Assembly of diplomatic mice
Because the carriage was an example
Of man's cruelty in the name of research.
The cat belonged to a behaviourist
And had been raised in an environment
Of only black horizontal lines. So
It saw my sprinting across the beach
To dismantle its harness as a whirl
Of fenceposts and orange rubber balls
And was gone faster than the better idea
You had a moment ago. Leaving me
Only the seagull's dreadful anthem:
'I just want to tell you how sad we all feel.'
The airplane trail made the cloud a wick—
I thought I saw it starting to burn down
And I knew we had been lucky to avoid
Disaster so far. I shared a bench with
A man who wanted to redefine us
As victims of one kind or another
Instead of whatever names we'd chosen:
Steven Victim, Jenny Victim, Franklin
Victim. I disagreed but couldn't speak.
He ate raw mushrooms from a paper bag.
In fact it was a computer game called
The Enormous Pointlessness of it All III.
When you are raised on computer games

You grow accustomed to saying 'I'm dead,'
Several times a day. Which is not to say
We are the first generation to feel
So comfortable with our mortality.

Four Neighbours

Four men live on my floor in the Edward Heath Memorial Building. The first, Patrick DeWitt, is tall and pale. His light-brown eyes and implacable mouth put you in mind of a seagull. He wears a tiny silver bucket on a chain around his neck and seems to take great pride in his appearance; his pinstripe suits are well-cut, his black hair is short and neat, but there is something sour in his expression—as if he suspects you think his appearance a sham. This man frequently loses his keys and is often seen remonstrating with the doorman who brilliantly feigns not to recognise him. His opinion of himself is so fragile that he must keep words of encouragement tacked to his wall in a disguised hand—elegant and light of touch so as to suggest a concerned lover. *Don't give up—you must trust yourself.*

The second, known to me only as Fenstermacher, is a pot-bellied lunatic with a hairy little round head like an otter. I sometimes think I can see steam rising off him. He is always gleeful and looking forward to something, but when he greets you cheerfully you should remember that this thing he is looking forward to is the £5 peepshow on the next road and that it is from this reserve of feather boas over rouged nipples and loose garter belts that his bonhomie is drawn. Before he cries—which he does little and often—his chin becomes as heavy as a mantelpiece and the effort to keep his mouth closed is such that his entire face puckers into the shape of a cat's bottom.

The third, Henry Caddy, has terrible posture and seems embarrassed to be alive. He is really a very stupid man: he looks at you as if you were about to lash out at him with your umbrella. When he talks his voice is thick and patchy, like a clarinet with a broken reed—and he stutters. His eyes are like an aerial view of two empty jars of peanut butter. He is a very allergic man, but never carries a handkerchief, preferring to run his hand up his nose, over his forehead and through his long, silky hair. He is stingy, but careless with money; just when you think you have him down as a glutton you see him emerging from the bookies, his green hat riding low on his forehead; later you may catch him accompanying his neighbour to the peepshow or placing a box of five empty sherry bottles outside his door: he cannot even apply himself to vice with any constancy.

I have never seen my fourth neighbour, Dr. Southernhay, only heavy doors closing behind him. However, I have read his column in *The Stern Utterance*, an obscure and unpopular evening newspaper printed in the Eastern Quarter on haddock-yellow paper. In this column, apparently lacking any nobler inspiration, he writes about his other neighbours with unbridled hostility. He describes me, for instance, as 'A scrawny lozenge-sucking deviant with a gamey smell,' and speaks of my tendency to lurk and stare at passers-by. 'No doubt he stays up long into the night playing with himself,' he concludes.

The Six Times My Heart Broke

The first time my heart broke was in an elephant graveyard. The elephant skulls looked like urinals with tusks. 'Why have you brought me to this elephant graveyard?' I asked. 'It's not working out,' she said. 'You love me more than I love you. I thought the elephant carcasses made a nice backdrop.'

The second time my heart broke was in the middle of the second take of an action sequence in a heist movie. 'That wasn't in the script,' I said to my co-star. 'I know,' she replied, and we cowered behind the car door for a series of controlled explosions.

The third time my heart broke I had my heart removed and replaced by a donor heart. I dipped my former heart into a container of liquid nitrogen and dropped it onto a paving slab where it smashed. 'Art project,' I explained to a pedestrian.

The fourth time my heart broke was when I swept up the shards of my frozen heart and carried them in a coolbox to a nearby gallery, but while I was chatting with the gallery owner, a dog used his nose to dislodge the coolbox lid and ate the heart. 'Maybe we could exhibit the turd,' suggested the gallery owner.

The fifth time my heart broke was when the dog turd that was once my heart was sealed in a glass container and purchased by an elite terrorist group, exhibited as an example of Western decadence—being an especially odious example of our cultural life—and used to recruit car bombers, one of whom obliterated my pen-pal while he was drafting a response to my overly-critical review of his first novel.

The sixth time my heart broke I was working out my donor heart by swimming laps in a crater full of rainwater. 'I have nothing to say,' said a boy standing at the edge of the crater. 'Or nobody wants to hear it, anyway.' I wanted to yell and tell him not to get discouraged, but I had swallowed a duck call and so could only quack. He left and never painted the triptych he was supposed to.

Bestiary For The Seven Days

Content, like a carnival, Monday stretches its long hair taut over its giant hollow eyes and plucks a rudimentary tune. The scientists are flicking salt at your boyfriend. They do not believe in the efficacy of occult practices, but maybe that's because they name every spark that flies from the lathe.

Bored, like a parade, Tuesday lies on the tracks, swallowing the trains as they approach its mouth and excreting them safely back onto the track moments later. The doctors are traumatised by what they have seen in the Penny Dreadful. They do not believe in the tyranny of photography, but only because they draw no distinction between art and the retina.

Exultant, like a procession, Wednesday dances on a pile of five-hundred fat dead bodies dressed in pinstripe suits; it is waving a sign which reads 'I AM THE COOLEST THING EVER!' The anthropologists are masturbating in the gazebo. They do not believe in despotic authoritarianism, but they are wrong to doubt our leaders who are doing the best they can in the circumstances.

Frightened, like a pageant, Thursday arranges antique dolls on the prow of a ship. The builders are catching tainted pilchards just off the coast of Minehead. They do not believe in divination by migratory geese, but one of them claims to have had lunch with Kahlil Gibran.

Claustrophobic, like a demonstration, Friday heats a tin of condensed milk over a camping stove and licks its lips. The dermatologists are reading Wittgenstein by the disued swimming pool. They do not believe in dance as political expression, but perhaps that's because we have to eat so much all the time that it's difficult to think about anything else.

Lonely, like a march, Saturday chews on a rolling pin. The writers are smashing one another over the head with marble clubs. They do not believe in contacting the dead, but maybe that's because most of them *are* dead.

Grateful, like a rally, Sunday peers at tiny green lights through the smoke in the clearing. The soldiers weep in the theatre courtyard. They do not believe in the healing properties of laughter, but then they have only ever laughed at their genitalia projected onto the sides of cathedrals.

Estate

The house is a giant aluminium tray.
There's a dried yellow residue on the walls,
A lingering smell of garlic. However,
The surface is so easy to clean —
And provided the next bus doesn't whip
The whole place away in its backdraft, I'm
Heading into town to buy some Sheen.
It *conducts* heat. I put on the immersion
And within minutes I can't even touch the walls.
Also I've got plans to put in a partition just there —
Because essentially it's a buy-to-let;
I'll be the live-in landlord. I'm looking for a young
Professional couple or a trainee journalist.
Or just anyone who doesn't mind me
Taping myself screaming through the night.

Wolf Nationalist

I

After studying the census the wolf discovers that he is exactly one quarter Welsh (maternal grandmother), one quarter English (maternal grandfather), one quarter Scottish (paternal grandmother) and one quarter Northern Irish (paternal grandfather).

'This raises all sorts of issues,' he says, solemnly. 'I'm not sure who I should be angriest with. Therefore I have decided to dedicate a day of the week to each. Mondays I am Welsh, Tuesdays Northern Irish, Wednesdays Scottish and Thursdays English. Friday is my day off having a nationality.'

'What about the weekends?' I ask.

'On the weekends I am American,' says the wolf. 'Because most of my favourite stuff is American: cheeseburgers, the music of the Byrds, Herman Melville and so on.'

'You can't just choose—'

'You English think you can tell everyone what to do,' snaps the Wolf. 'Well it won't do. The time of your hegemony is finally at an end. Except on Thursdays.'

II

It is Monday. The wolf strides up and down wearing a red Chinese dragon suit, swinging a cane and singing, 'As long as we physically assault the English.'

'It's *beat* the English,' I say. 'As in beat them at games.'

'That's not how I interpret it,' says the wolf. 'And it's about time my people had more of a say in how things are interpreted. My ancestors have been oppressed by yours for centuries.'

'If you want to get teleological,' I snap, 'I think you'll find my ancestors did no more than taylor or skivvy or make gravestones for the ancestors who oppressed *your* ancestors.'

'Balls,' says the wolf. 'Your ancestors should have found out what was going on and seized power in a humourless coup.'

'Bloodless coup,' I say.

'Blood is one of the humours,' says the wolf.

III

'Fortunately my mother was Opus Dei and my father a Methodist,' says the wolf. 'Thus, on Tuesdays, I am Catholic in the mornings and Protestant in the afternoons.'

'And at night?'

'I become Scottish at midnight,' says the wolf, 'so that's simple: I return to my Presbytarian roots. But between eight pm and eleven fifty-nine I'm an atheist.'

'It all feels a bit tokenistic,' I say.

'Oh and I suppose you can see inside my head and judge the weight of my convictions, can you?' spits the wolf. 'How like an Englishman. Let me assure you: whatever it is I'm supposed to be believing at the time, I believe it fully and without question. If I doubt there is a God, I pray for faith; and when I'm an atheist, should I doubt that there *isn't* a God, I hold my head in my hands and wait for the faith to pass.'

At lunchtime I find him drinking a cocktail of Bushmills and Jamesons, thumbing through a clothing catalogue.

'This national dress business is much more complicated than I first thought,' he says. 'For instance, bagpipes, kilts and short-bread were originally Irish. Yet now they are seen as quintessentially Scottish. Do I pander to stereotype or historical accuracy?'

'Depends who you're trying to impress,' I say.

'A *very* English thing to say,' mutters the wolf.

IV

The wolf releases a box of midges into the house. 'It makes me feel at home,' he announces, scratching his arms, feverishly.

Two hours later I find him slumped in the corner with a mangled edition of *Crossways* and a bottle of cachaça.

'Drinking before noon again,' I say, putting the empty bottle of cachaça by the fridge with the others. 'Correct me if I'm wrong, but this nationalism business just seems to be an excuse to get drunk all the time.'

'Piss off, limey,' the wolf slurs.

'And cachaça?'

'The Scottish enjoy a special relationship with Latin America,' says the wolf. 'If you check the archives you'll find *Things Fall Apart* was best received by Scottish literary critics.'

'Chinua Achebe is Nigerian,' I say.

'You should know,' says the wolf. 'You colonised them.'

No Stars

At that time it was customary to wear a complete adult human skeleton around one's neck, which made moving house harder than ever and embracing almost impossible. There was a wild panic to the blue sky. The clack of our skeletons as we leant in to embrace, until we came to associate affection with clacking. But still we dated.

And of course had I known my own family had been abducted earlier that afternoon and were concurrently undergoing torments similar to that which it depicted, I mightn't have enjoyed the film so much.

Towards the end of the second act the torturer offers his victims ice cream and popcorn while they watch him 'work', which I thought was clever and funny.

But maybe a bit too clever. And I didn't like the inverted commas around 'work'—it made me want to say the word 'vomit' in inverted commas.

I felt the urge to explain it to the rest of the cinema. 'We are implicated just by observing!' I whispered to my date, who looked up from her copy of Empire—which described the film as 'a sadistic circle-jerk of the lowest order.'

She took my shoulders and kissed me on the forehead.

'Peace,' she muttered.

The police had filled my house with graphic photographs of the crime scene. _____ __ _____ _____ _____ __ __, _____ __ ___ _____ ___ ____. ___ _ ___ _ _____ _____.[1] When I complained, they told me I was entitled to my opinion. As I sprinkled instant coffee granules into our cups of real coffee,

(a post-structural drink I liked to call ""THE SIMULACRA BESEIGED!' "")

I reflected that the torturer had taught me a valuable lesson which, on closer inspection, turned out to be a cliché:

The last crisp in the bowl is a rat who has eaten the last crisp in the bowl.

1 Should you ever feel sickened by your own thoughts, take a moment to pity those who spend millions of pounds and enlist the help of thousands of technical experts to realise their own sickening thoughts in a form that can be inflicted on millions of others. You are, let's be honest, not that bad.

Pleasure Beach

The pilgrim sits on a rock
Reading *Thus Spake Zarathustra*.

'Know your enemy,' I say, approvingly.
'*Love* your enemy,' he corrects. 'Prick.'

I buy a stick of rock from the ghost pier—
A mistake I often make—

All the way through it is written
THE DEAD THANK YOU. And then

Two boys in computerised spectacles
Burst their dinghy against the harbour.

Their computerised spectacles are no use,
Offering them, as they drown,

A cut-rate on a 12 megapixel camera—
With which one might take a photo of the harbour

From the crumbling hills and zero-in
On their faces as they thrash around

Without any limitation to picture quality.
I am laughing—

Because the Category Assessment Form
I have to fill in to report the accident

Is abbreviated to CAT ASS.
'Do you think that's funny?' I ask the pilgrim.

'Cat ass,' he chuckles. 'Yeah, that's funny.'
The pilgrim and I have the same sense of humour.

The birds look like numbers.
The sea is sentimental.

I sell three paperweights to an overweight
Anglican minister who asks me

Why I'm surrounded by moth-winged devils,
How much I know about the counter-reformation,

Then he runs out of the fossil shop, whooping.
Later children armed with bicycle chains

Steal my trousers and throw them in the sea.
The criminal psychologists lend the place

Its unmistakable drinking-to-forget vibe.
Ours is the only coastal town

To feature an exact copy of our coastal town
In bronze, actual size, two miles down the road.

Army

Dear mum and dad, I expect,
With all the paint falling out of the sky,
You thought I'd forgotten you.
Wrong! I detect your presence
In the exuberance and wit of deciduous trees!

Last week we had to fling a wall over a wall,
But we got the wrong wall:
We flung the wall over the wall
We were supposed to fling over the wall
We flung over that wall. It's difficult to explain

And I have no great facility with language—
My eloquence marred, perhaps,
By my curtailed education.
Thank you for *Seven Types of Ambiguity*
And the box of brandy snaps;

I'm afraid I don't understand either of them.

Wolf on the Couch

I.

'WHO LIVES IN YOUR HEAD?' the wolf bellows.

The wolf has completed a correspondence course in psycho-analysis and is testing it out on me.

'Nobody,' I say. I am lying on the floor in his new office — to which he invited me on the pretext of 'a nice drink'.

'Nonsense,' says the wolf, striding up and down the room. 'Some-one or something lives in everyone's head. Who lives in yours?'

'There is one thing,' I say, trying to stop the points of light pitch-ing and rolling. 'I have created an alter-ego through whom I voice opinions I am not brave enough to voice myself and whom I also use for self-censure and masochism.'

'Hmm,' says the wolf, his pen scratching across his Psychologist's Jotter. 'Sounds more like an alter-superego. Describe him.'

II.

'He's an owl,' I say.

'Preposterous,' splutters the wolf. 'What does he look like?'

'Squat, tawny, beakish,' I say. 'When you look closely he appears to be made up of a network of tiny cities.'

'And in the rain?'

'The same, but wetter.'

'And all the people in these tiny cities,' says the wolf, 'do they run for buses when the owl is wet? The men with their black umbrellas, the women with their Nancy Mitford novels held over their coconut-scented heads, the light in the city like an old grey ice cream?'

'You'd need a microscope to see that,' I mutter.

'And is there a pretty young woman with sheer black tights who is running also?'

'Annabelle,' I say.

'Excellent.' The wolf continues to write for several minutes. An ambulance siren in the street below—ambulances have always sounded like a mean little boy shouting, 'Weirdo! Weirdo!'

'This owl you keep mentioning,' says the wolf, finally. 'I'm going to need some details: his political persuasion, his school reports, sexual preferences, favourite foods, his accent, his attitude to authority figures and so forth.'

'He doesn't tell me that sort of thing,' I mutter. 'His accent is like a pair of shears.'

'Then we'd better ask him,' says the wolf. 'In those cities in the rain, are there also television studios?'

III.

The owl sits in a red velvet chair, his shirt rakishly unbuttoned to the middle. The wolf has his legs crossed in the presenter's manner. The theme tune is all twenty-eight and a half minutes of Mozart's *Piano Concerto No. 21 in C major*. The wolf becomes increasingly impatient. Finally the audience's applause ebbs away and the wolf is able to turn to the owl and say:

'Religion, nationality and profession.'

'Presbyterian, Ruritanian and Sancitmonium,' replies the owl in a maddening falsetto.

'Favourite colour, novel and point of reference,' says the wolf.

'Presbyterian, Ruritanian and Sancitmonium,' replies the owl.

The wolf blanches, stands up, his shoulders tensing, trying very hard to compose himself. He closes his eyes.

'Political persuasion, football team and sexual preference,' he whispers, tearfully.

'Presbyterian, Ruritanian and Sancitmonium,' replies the owl.

The wolf howls, picks up the owl, shakes him and tears him to pieces, finding him full of yellow and orange fluff and a small tape-recorder playing, 'Presbyterian, Ruritanian and Sancitmonium,' on a loop. The audience applauds.

~

'You dastard!' cries the wolf, back in the office. 'You set me up!'

'You can't interview the owl when you're *on* the owl,' I say. 'I mean, you *can't*, can you? It would be like trying to suck a vacuum cleaner into itself.'

The wolf stands and writes ORALLY FIXATED on a white board in the shape of a giant pair of lips.

IV.

The wolf has asked me to complete a list of phrases making each set-of-three phonetically similar to the last. 'It is a technique known as Sharking for Snow,' he says. Within ten minutes I have filled in the sheet.

It wounds me to see you flying like that —
I always want to accuse you of something:
Your failure to scrutinise the clouds. [1]

Baboons need to feel the sighing white flat [2]
Hallways daunt and confuse, hooves thumping:
Regalia, while Putinised, astounds. [3]

Marooned, we pursue the Olympiad,
The 'Four Ways' haunt Syracuse [4] *like a dumpling —* [5]
Pygmalion has notified the crowds. [6]

Next we take a long walk around the city park, looking up at the office window, looking down at the yellow leaves. Leaning against the gazebo, a blues guitarist thumps his guitar.

'It is a *tour de weakness*,' says the wolf.

---

[1] The wolf is pleased. 'Already you are working out some deep-seated feelings,' he says. 'Jealousy, entropy, Feudalism.'
'That's *your* stanza,' I say. 'I didn't write any of that.'
'All the same,' says the wolf. 'A good poem is a good poem, no matter who wrote it.'

[2] At this the wolf flies into a rage. 'What exactly is that supposed to mean?' he yells. 'Firstly you ruin all of your hard work by mentioning an *ape* — calling card of the imaginatively constipated — then you mix two metaphors that never existed in the first place: I'll allow you that a flat can sigh, a *white* flat all the better, but that a baboon is even *capable* of

feeling, let alone that he *depends* on the sighing of a flat for his very life is just stupid. Make it a "balloon" instead.'

3 'Very religious,' comments the wolf.

4 'The city of Syracuse, New York, was founded on an ancient Indian burial ground,' says the wolf. 'I can only assume that these "Four Ways" are the four ways of the ancients: hunting, meditation, dance and laughter.'

5 'The way a dumpling haunts a stew,' the wolf observes, 'Floating, on the surface and yet dense and heavy. Excellent.'

6 'About what?' says the wolf. 'You can't just leave it there! What does Pygmalion want the crowds to know? Something about Galatea, presumably. Then tell us! We *are* the crowds!'

'There wasn't any room.' I complain.

'A proper writer would have *made* room,' says the wolf.

V.

'All superheroes are essentially giant phalluses,' says the wolf. 'If you were a superhero, which would you be? Batman, Spiderman or Superman?'

'Batman,' I say.

The wolf writes, THINKS PENIS IS A BAT on the whiteboard.

I am back on the couch now, trying to keep still.

'Now for the Rorschach test,' says the wolf, picking up a pile of white cards.

On each card the wolf has daubed black and red ink.

'They're supposed to be butterfly paintings,' I say.

'What?' snaps the wolf.

'I mean they're supposed to be symmetrical,' I say. 'You're supposed to paint one side and fold it over.'

'Fascinating,' says the wolf and writes, BELIEVES EVERYTHING SHOULD MAKE SENSE on the whiteboard. 'A fine sentiment from a man who thinks his penis is a bat,' he adds.

VI.

'Here's my diagnosis,' says the wolf. 'You want life to be episodic, to have a clear beginning and end like a film or a novel. Whereas real life is far more amorphous than that—as any film or novel will tell you.'

'That's not true,' I say.

'See?' says the wolf. 'A conclusive statement, as always. The only cure is Word Disassociation. I say a word, you reply with a word that has absolutely nothing to do with it. Fish,' says the wolf.

'Disappointment,' I say.

'Ointment,' says the wolf.

'Larch,' I say.

'Tribe,' says the wolf.

'Inflation,' I say.

This goes on for two hours, during which the wolf systematically undoes every synapse.

'There,' he announces. 'How do you feel now?'

'Pointed,' I say.

'Excellent,' says the wolf.

'Xylophone,' I say.

'Then I'll see you this time next week,' says the wolf.

'Hottentots,' I say.

Grapefruit

I was ashamed of the ways of my household:
The tame bear dressed in a ball gown;
My brothers' Hitler moustaches;
Father's pre-dinner 'Stomach Opera'

Which seemed longer than usual that evening;
(Never was I more relieved that my work on the libretto
Had gone unacknowledged)
The way mother shook legs instead of hands.

When asked if he preferred *pomelo* or *shaddock*
My lover replied that either was lovely—
'True! For they are both grapefruit!' cried Steven,
Then answered every question with 'Mandibles.'

All night his nervous laughter was a blizzard,
Even when Marcus asked him to pass the 'boring'
And I kicked Marcus under the table
And he kicked me right back again and we giggled.

We all knew it was a disposable suit and tie,
But how supercilious he must have thought us.
'I should bait your hook with a few grim realities,'
He muttered, leaving before port, before *pudding*,

For the ship that would convey him hence;
And how are we to live with irrelevance?
We mowed him down in the Silver Ghost,
Bludgeoned him with a globe.

Childhood

I remember the look on your face when I said,
'All is born out of boredom: Mud is boredom.'
And how I was sent in search of my room—
I found it under the reflection of my face.

Our community was divided into cooperative factions;
Friendly but guarded, like a dolphin's smile.
If you were an animist, you could marry a plinth.
The morning our flag was redesigned to incorporate

More flashing lights, I watched fireworks
Exploding against a blue sky.
I had just learned how to say the word, 'Koan'.
The air was thick with hatred. I barricaded

The doors. My sister picked up the golden banjo;
I told her to pick up something less fragile.
While we argued over suitable weapons
The door was broken down and our mother screamed.

Oversized men tore through the house,
Chucking father into the samovar.
They were dressed in sharp things;
It was an advertisement, but not for sharp things.

It was for some kind of waffle-shaped cake.
It is a fact of life in every neighbourhood:
You can't play a piano under water, but
You can ride the concept of a horse forever.

When I rounded the corner a pile of waiting rooms
Lay in ambush, chanting 'Spare us the homily.'
The boy with glue on his jumper made bats
By paperclipping moths to the backs of mice.

He left them at the foot of my bed, offerings,
Like he was my cat. I did my best to detach him,
But we remained friends until he joined the army—
Or what he *thought* was the army;

It was actually just one of many armies.
A local clown ran a seminary for balancing acts:
'To do something hilariously wrong
You must first learn to do it better than an expert.

A clown requires a momentary tableau of lyrical beauty
Before plates, chairs and animals come crashing down.'
My father was mortified when I questioned his police work.
Through rigorous training, the child learns

To appear still whilst expending furious effort.
Several things make even less sense in retrospect:
Did radio presenters *really* interrupt their shows to talk to me?
Did the sun actually set three times that night at the beach?

How could the mortician tell me everything would be alright?
What was with the man who painted roadside imaginary
        topless women to cause car accidents?
The gold aeroplane I saw circling our house?
Why was it only the children in duffle coats who died?

My First Impulse is <u>Always</u> to Take the Bigger Portion, the Unchipped Cup, the Cleaner Glass

i.m

When I heard the denizens of the paladium say that suicide was selfish and weak I prayed that they would suffer. Which was an evil thing to pray for. How to love even them? At least, anyway, their hearts will split open like seed-pods, one day, same as the rest of us. Because all life is a splitting open. But I can't. I want them to suffer *now*. Plane passes overhead on the note that begins a long, sad film.

The Awakening

Nothing, it seems, will appease the giant eye.
It is roughly the size of a hot-tub. It winks sporadically.

The iris is a light, deciduous green. It lies in the city square.
Excavations to find the rest of the face have uncovered nothing.

Several theories exist as to the giant eye's implication.
'*Challenge received ideology!*' is one.

'*Challenge the credulous goons who think
They're challenging received ideology!*'

Is another. It has also become popular to say,
'The only reason you'd object is if you had something to hide.'

Salt and remonstration have failed.
The newspapers: WE'RE ALL GOING TO BE SORRY.

Today they are building a wall around the giant eye.
A crowd gathers. The thunder applauds them.

Painful Revisions
for a doctor

Today is your birthday, doctor: Communal singing in the streets;
Fireworks over the hospital: Is everyone cured?

Everyone's cured, right? That's great!
Everyone is cured, once and for all.

Thank you for curing me. I always forget to thank you,
Just like nobody thinks of umbrellas on a sunny day.

But the fireman thanks you with plumes of water;
The ballerina thanks you by stressing the purity and harmony
    of design;

The ballerina thanks you by striving for something
So beautiful it does not seem to belong to this world.

Today I am wearing my ice skates to the hospital
Because all buildings and actions are identical to me.

How sad to have *chosen* sadness, as I now realise I did:
I can pinpoint the exact day, if you'd like.

The Forms Of Despair

We returned from the war happier, arms around our shadows—
Who claimed to be older than us. They told great jokes

Lay around barefoot, hair precisely
Unkempt, cigarettes hissing and glowing like christmas lights.

Only our fiancées were tired and bothersome,
Having forgotten how to love, or vice versa.

Some had moved to factories in other cities,
Others, when pressed, said, 'No-one's forcing you to put up with me.'

We went skating with our shadows,
Huddled under fir trees drinking sausage tea.

Inquisitive sheep collected around our camp;
It was good to be among the ice storm and the believers.

We described the funny pages to Simon—who had lost both his eyes
But the jokes didn't work so well in description.

Repetition

Tomorrow is a process. Our neighbours are cruel
And I keep cutting myself on the new knives—
What am I to make of all the repetition?

A virtue? I know everything already;
If the barrier is made of ice, you wait for it to melt—
But what am I to make of all the repetition?

Music? I have carpeted the inside of the piano;
The dog won't bite you if you bite it first—
But what am I to make of all the repetition?

A system? I lack the education to understand
The insults being levelled at me. My nose fell off—
And what am I to make of all the repetition?

A matchstick longboat? Under the circumstances
I cannot see the point of a matchstick longboat.
What am I to make of all the repetition?

Humility? A divining-rod? Uncreated light?
I do not understand my own laughter.
Tell me what I am to make of all the repetition.

Wilful obscurantism? An obsolete pigment?
Far too much depends on this board-game—
An agreeable ritual made of repetition.

Lunch is ready. My loved-ones are plotting against me,
Locks appear everywhere. Why am I so angry?
What am I to make of all the repetition?

A Terrorist, Maybe, With His Children

The most miserable crustacean is the crab
With his eyes like juniper berries on sticks,
His eyes like a junior doctor trying to give you bad news.
I hate his little humourless claw, and also his big claw:
He is an action hero miscast in a romantic comedy
(The sea is a romantic comedy).
His mouth is like nervous fingers, or a hungry biomechanical coin slot;
Movement in a flat, still plane—a terrorist, maybe, with his children.
He walks sideways, like a man who's just made an offensive joke
Sidles out of the conversation to get another mojito.
Maybe you will say 'No! The crab is magnificently humble!
His eyes are like buttons on a shiny new console
which will control a lightshow for a charity function.'
It would be such a shame if the crab failed due to total lack of interest.

The Last Days of Advertising

I. THE MIGRAINE HOTEL

It was one of those bashed-in silver nights;
A sense of work unfinished like an itch
In the very centre of your head.

H. sat in a cloud at the bar drinking
The stagnant English beer we hated,
His thoughts flicking away like shrimp.

Lead us not into television, was one of them.
He translated it into words and spoke it.
That night we heard him through the wall

Praying, 'God, I am nowhere. Or I am clawing
My way up a column of something fleshy—
I think it might be my own mouth.

I think I live in my own mouth. Please send money.'
We agreed: H. had become an empty signifier;
Although none of us could agree what that meant.

A registered trademark or a blimp or whatever.
Really, the end-credits approached all of us;
Our qualifications were not recognised

By the new administration—as if the cat
Walking over the board game was the context
And not, as we had thought, the boardgame.

'And we are just toppled pieces,' he murmured.
'Those nights we stayed up worrying we were frauds:
Now we may see them as our only real work—

The diagnosis of our own fraudulence.
Tell me,' he said, 'what is the German for:
I never even learned a second language?'

II. AS THE MENU IS TO FOOD

The sky was violently blue.
Never a good sleeper, H. had constructed
A paperclip mausoleum the size of his hotel room.
For breakfast he thought about fear,
How it underpins everything like toothache.
We awaited our arrest.

Further evidence of his brilliant downfall:
He has struck-through every line in his diaries
(1968–2008) and written, in the final margin,
Cliché. So where next in our sparkling
Hangover? To Tuesday, inexorably.
Each day an ocean with imagined liners.

This house H. imperfectly inhabited,
Dreaming every night of a former house.
H. sat on the place like a sticker,
Like a word misused for years,
Listened to the saws panting next door.
The mice are our footnotes.[1]

---

[1] [Squeak, scrabble-scrabble-scrabble, sounds of eating, etc.]

The 30-second spot comprising a slow pan across a graveyard, and a bi-plane, skywriting, as the camera closes in on a gravestone inscribed simply, YOU, before focusing on a close-up of an abandoned can of Coke at the side of 'your' gravestone, spilled slightly over the ground, closer still to reveal an ant paddling with one foot at the surface of a brown droplet on a blade of grass before we pan out again to reveal the skywriter has written the following:

Coca-Cola predates you . . .
. . . and will outlast you!

Followed by a slow fade to the familiar cursive, this time not in skywriting, but superimposed over the scene in white:

And there is absolutely nothing
you can do about it!

H.'s original catch-phrase was over 17,000 words long, divided into chapters and concerned, among other things, our living 'outside of history' a state blamed by H. largely on Coca-Cola itself. One chapter entitled 'We Are History's Exoskeleton', which digresses on the theme of exoskeletons *per se* and the 'kingdoms of insects' about which we know 'Not nearly so much as we think we do, nor ever will.'

Like much of the tagline, this was considered excessive by the junior copy-editor who simply took the first and last sentences of the thesis and came up with the graveyard scenario by herself, which enraged H., (who refused to attend the awards ceremony at which the commercial was later honoured), but then so did everything at that point, enrage him.

Yet he recalls this time fondly in his autobiography.

[46]

IV. HE DOESN'T LOVE ANYWHERE ELSE, EITHER

The street is paved with human teeth,
Set in cement, like little white and yellow cobblestones —
Looks like a giant ivory snake.
The cottage is thatched with his own hair.
That's where H. lives and where all of his telescopes are.
It's such a terrible town people brag about having lived there:

'I saw a whole *group* of men smoking
Through their tracheotomy holes! A group!
Like it was a conference of tracheotomy-hole-smokers!'
And 'Here the babies push their *mothers* in prams!'
Which is presumably a crack about underage mothers.
But he lives there because he is authentic.

He doesn't love it, the town, like a monkey
Presumably doesn't *love* trees. Anyway,
How could you say you *loved* that place
Out of anything other than journalist-baiting bombast?
In no way, that's how. So he doesn't *love* the town,
But he stays because he doesn't love anywhere else, either.

A Dog Descends

Before I was born the seer predicted, 'You will be inaudible in the laughter of many doctors.'

When I was born they tied a red ribbon around my ankle and glued fur onto my back so that my blind father could tell the difference between me and the dog—a hairless breed. This didn't work as the fur just wouldn't stay on, so I had to learn to touch-type whilst drinking from a dog bowl and sleeping amid the scraps. Mother kept saying, 'Father knows best.' When I protested, father would scream, 'WILL SOMEONE SHUT UP THAT INFERNAL TALKING DOG?' When the dog barked or whimpered, my father would shout, 'WILL SOMEONE TEACH THAT INFERNAL BOY TO SPEAK?'

And gradually the dog picked up a thing or two; leftovers, mostly; things I didn't need to say that often, observations about Wordsworth's late style and the plasticity of nationalism. Stuff I wasn't going to need as I wasn't going to university. Experts were brought in to teach the dog more. Soon it could say, 'The sight of the real mountains usurped upon Wordsworth's imagining of the mountains; which is to say, gobbled them up.' And I started talking less and less and just enjoying some meat, the taste of which, you might say, usurped upon the idea of meat.

David Jones, the underrated Welsh poet and artist, remained my own personal territory, and, as I had been smuggled a laptop by a friendly aunt, I was able to work on my dissertation to keep from going completely insane. Father took me out for walks, marvelling at my talent as a guide dog, and kicking me in the side whenever I tried to start a conversation.

Mother would buy me dog treats and, sometimes, as a treat, human treats like books and spectacles. Tragedy came next, like unexpected sunlight through a dirty window: a psychiatrist got hold of my David Jones essay and analysed it for latent content, finding that it revealed a disturbing relationship between myself and my parents.

So I was relocated to the dog's parents. They lived in a barn in some hay. They spent their days licking me in the eye and barking. I was expected to go out and maybe kill a rabbit or a badger and if I returned with no kill, my new dog parents would snarl and bite me. What a life. My new name was Goujon and the farmers all laughed at this amazing intelligent dog. They took me to market sometimes and got me to do tricks like talking about Jones's exemplary use of secondary citation in *The Sleeping Lord*.

Meanwhile every night I slept in yesterday's newspapers, from which I came to learn that my father's dog was enjoying a fine new career in academia, proselytising on Dryden (of all people), and was popular with his colleagues and students alike. 'It's as if,' he was reported to say, but then my dog father pissed on the article and it dissolved before I could finish it.

One cold Wednesday my dog parents both became sick and I was able to enjoy an independent week, away from their constant demands. I walked on my hind-legs right out of the barn and joined a travelling side-show as 'Goujon the Human Faced and Bodied and Brained Dog!' I was popular, but not, I'm afraid to say, as anything other than a novelty. I fed on peanut brittle cakes and candyfloss, avoided the spite of the clowns and soon fell in love with my female counterpart, 'Jennifer the Rabbit who Looks and Behaves Exactly Like a Woman!' We decided we would start a new life in Switzerland, maybe. Open a petrol station—because no-one ever aspires to opening a petrol station and they're probably very lucrative.

The problem was money: our wages paid our cage rental, food rations and 'protection' from the other circus acts. So we'd have to get proper jobs. We gradually befriended the circus master over the course of two years—until he trusted us enough to leave our cages open at night; whereupon we absconded, caught a slow train to the next county and took a bed-sit in the low-rent district.

Jennifer trained as a teacher and I took a job as a life-insurance salesman, trying to work out when people were going to die and placing high-stakes bets with them that they wouldn't. Frankly, this doomed gambling with death itself wasn't much better than the circus. And my diet of fairground sweets had left me severely malnourished and in need of constant dental attention—which was costly to say the least.

Within five years we had saved nothing and my 50-CD Swedish language course lay in its plastic wallets behind the bread-bin, with the Usborne Guide to Running a Petrol Station, covered in crumbs. However, we had moved from the low-rent district to a small ground-floor flat with a garden. Jennifer was a fully qualified history teacher when she—or we—became pregnant. I tried to call my father to share the good news, but he just yelped and hung up. Next time I dialled the number the operator told me it had been disconnected. I hadn't heard anything about the dog in a while. I assumed he was dead of old age by now.

Late one night while Jennifer lay sleeping, I went into our garden and looked up at the stars. I had not kept the garden in very good shape and it had been taken over by brambles, but I didn't care about that tonight. A wild rose had forced its way through in the corner. I stood there, breathing. A big white cat sat on our disused shed, staring at me. I like cats—because they seem to be as confused as we are.

Addiction Clinic

Subject A is aroused by people brushing their teeth. He likes to watch people brushing their teeth, okay? It's the only thing that gets him going, if you understand me. I mean can you imagine that? The *only thing*. He has—I don't know—a *periscope* or something and he uses it to watch people, in this *bathroom* he hired, brushing their teeth. But get this: he likes the tooth-brusher to be *fully aware* that he's watching them. He's not a voyeur; I mean he wouldn't care about just watching some complete stranger who didn't know he was watching them brush their teeth. That would do nothing for him—he finds the idea laughable. No. He rents a flat in the opposite building to his, one that has a bathroom facing his living-room window, and then he hires someone —every night it's a different person—to spend twenty minutes in that bathroom, brushing their teeth—on the understanding that he's going to be watching them through his *periscope*, or whatever the hell it is, the whole time. What he likes is this. It's that the tooth-brusher—who he has hired and paid in advance —must *act the role* of somebody un-self-consciously brushing their teeth. That's what he's paying them for—and they go along with it: the guy's a sicko. Whatever. But they're wrong—it's not the watching-someone-who-doesn't-know-it thing: he's not a voyeur. It's the exact opposite. He's got people standing at this sink in an uninhabited apartment thinking, 'Well, I guess I'd better brush my teeth as naturally as possible so he gets his money's worth.' And it's in doing that, in that *striving*, in the agony of consciously trying to be un-self-aware as they brush their teeth, that the tooth-brusher reveals something of themselves. A *glint*, you know, nothing blatant, but a glint. That's what this guy's into: glints.

BEAUTIFUL

Subject B was a beautiful girl, really beautiful—and I know that's sort of inappropriate of me to say so in my position, but c'mon! I'm human, just like you are, right? We all have the same weaknesses. Or, rather, most of us do. You know what Subject B liked? She liked to go to the beach and start fights. She'd wear this sort of ridiculous harlequin costume—and this was kind of a personal case for me because I've always hated harlequins—she'd wear the costume, and it was a really tacky, spangly sort of a harlequin costume, she'd go to the beach and then she'd wander about *kicking sand in children's faces*. The really dry sand, you know? Dune sand. Now, you understand human nature as well as I do, I hope: if someone kicks sand in your child's face, you're going to be pretty cross about it. So she'd get these furious parents yelling at her, 'Why the hell did you do that?' and 'Are you completely in*sane*?' And that's when she liked to go to pieces. Just throw herself on the sand, weeping and screaming how sorry she was. And sometimes the family would just leave in disgust, but sometimes they'd actually be quite sympathetic. They'd start asking her what was wrong, give her a cup of tea, try to help her. A lot of people are pretty fucking nice when it comes down to it. Yeah, I know you think it's unacceptable—but in a way, isn't Subject B the only one who's being honest here? Most of us have to find *really subtle ways* of kicking sand in our friends' children's faces. Most of us do exactly what she does and we totally get away with it! That's the moral you can learn from these freaks, usually.

JUDGEMENT

You've got to understand that I'm not judging anyone here—I mean, hell, whatever gets you through this horrible world. I eat a lot of crisps and make up fake personas on internet dating forums—so I'm hardly beyond reproach, that's what I'm saying. What I think is if you call someone weird, *you're* weird. It's as simple as that. But this one guy, let's call him Subject D, gets *turned on by judging people*. I know! He forms partisan, subjective opinions about people and expresses them eloquently to anyone who'll listen. He's pretty persuasive, too. I've been won over by him on several occasions. He's a well-educated man—you ever meet one of those? Yeah, they can be pretty snooty, but he, you know, he's alright. He doesn't look down on you—except for when he's judging you, naturally. Now, I'm the last one to judge someone for being judgemental—I'm pretty judgemental myself, so I'm not going to start getting on any high horse here. I'm not going to cast the first stone. But I can tell you, after talking to this guy for several weeks, what he *really* gets off on is not the judging *per se*, but the *exponential judgmentalism* it inspires in others. It's like when you blow a dandelion and release all the little white parachute spores. That's kind of the moneyshot for him.

Five Poems For A New Shopping Centre

I. THE MAUDLIN BALUSTRADES

Where peacocks mount statues of peacocks
And stagger away astounded with chipped beaks
I put on my blindfold and ran as fast as I could.
My psychiatrist says I can't liken you to an ant-farm,
So I liken you to my heart, shoes my red blood cells.
Our bodies coincide into a bait-ball and we absorb
The nimbus of silvery light where a god hailed a taxi.
Policemen walk home in tears without their shoes.
Everything is a special offer until eventually
Not getting a callous and sarcastic comment
Or not getting tweaked on the nose is a special offer.
The smiles of the stuffed animals are knowing,
Scared, too. I fling myself into a glass obelisk
Where you may purchase this and other titles.

II. HOLES!

You are filled with giant holes that make us secretly want to jump! Doyenne of the inner maniac, holes more sublime than a cathedral! You should consider changing your name to *The Holes*! I will if you will! It is our most remarkable feature!

You are shot through with holes! Replete with holes, as my work is with violence! BANG! See? My eye takes in every shop from every floor when I am in you! But what captures the eye most is the holes themselves! Like a performance artist drawing attention to the act of 'performance'.

The eye plunges through your holes like a great bear losing its footing on a waterfall! Your ever blessed holes! I will drop household appliances into them! Will they ever be filled? No! I will drop items of clothing and shoes! I will drop laptops and Blackberries® and high-definition TVs!

Who can measure your holes? There is no tape measure long enough! The tape measures have fallen into you! I too, headfirst toward stone frogs! The girl from the candle store picks up pieces of my crunchylicious skull! Lo, there is no end! Lo, There is no beginning! Hooray!

III. YOUR DESIGNERS FEEL SAD SOMETIMES

Your designers feel sad sometimes
In ancient grey mornings,
Their coffee too weak or too strong.
They blink in their long thin gardens.
The dew seeps into their moccasins.
Their legs hurt.

IV. LETTER FROM SNOW

Dear shopping centre,

I don't usually write to anything, but I feel that you are making a horrible mistake: Can you hear the starling cackle as if charged by the electric high-wire it perches on? As the dove betokens peace, so the starling municipality. I digress, which is something you just *don't do*, hence my concern.

Yours sincerely,

Snow

V. MY FAKE ERUDITION

The ancient king was cursed and turned into a jar of honey.
The Prime Minister himself dug the drainage basin.
The courtiers were renowned for their dislike of the letter K.

My darling, when they awarded the award,
At least you were honest enough to declare you didn't understand.
Honesty is going to be more prized than any award,

Even if someone is honestly a complete shit.
Your frosted glass reminds us of that.
You are a dozen stupid castles,

We are exhausted kings and queens
Playing chess with our grey, salivating dogs.
It's been their move for centuries.

A Sure-Fire Sign

Erica has a crazy idea that it's a redundant medium.

'Look at the very first page!' she says, tears in her eyes. 'You can't start with a film that doesn't exist—that's a sure-fire sign! 'I went to see a film that didn't exist . . .' Garbage. Garbage!'

My face goes hot. I stand up and look around the room for my clothes and begin to regret splitting the pill with her.

'At *this* time!' she says. 'In *this* country!'

A brass band passes our apartment. They sound like the mating call of a horrible amphibian.

'It's so comfortable,' she says. 'Bourgeois, even. You're like a fat little dog. You ought to have more pressing matters to attend to.'

I find my trousers behind Erica's cello.

'But you don't.'

At this point Erica is openly crying and I am looking away and crying.

'Just bad jokes about films-within-fucking-films that don't exist. I mean, what would you do if someone asked you to write something for their funeral?'

'I'd write something nice,' I say.

'See?' she says. 'You don't even care about the aesthetic! You abandon it at the first sign of resistance!'

∼

The crisis began with my latest project—a funeral for irony. The rites included a full church service and burial and a marble headstone engraved with

IRONY
? ?–2006
A LOVING RHETORICAL DEVICE AND TENDENCY

The funeral expenses amounted to three months rent—which means that we are now struggling.

~

I go to my patron. He keeps a caged bird named after each of the artists in his patronage. Mine is a little red parrot.

'Erica is being horrible to me,' I say.

'You should write a poem about her,' he says, addressing the parrot. 'Make her look stupid.'

The parrot gnaws on a beech nut.

'She'll just say it's bourgeois,' I say.

～

Situations under which my writing would be less bourgeois:

If I hadn't the money to eat as much as I wanted;
If I had been sectioned;
If I didn't have a house;
If I were uncomfortable with my sexuality;
If I were suffering religious persecution;
If I were woefully inarticulate;
If I were not allowed to go ice-skating every morning;
If I were a prisoner of the state;
If I were interested in disrupting the relationship between
        writer and reader;
If I expunged capital letters and punctuation;
If I stopped trying to be funny;
If I were to go on a pilgrimage;
If my sole motivation were not vanity.

≈

'For instance,' says Erica, 'I have a rule in my writing that I'm not allowed to use the following words: WRITING, POETRY, WRITER, POET, WRITTEN, NOVELIST, POEM, JOURNALIST, DRAMATIST, DIARIST. And whenever I do, I pull out one of my fingernails and dip the finger into a bowl of vinegar.'

≈

When the little red parrot dies, my patron will forget me and I will have to seek employment or state sponsorship.

'Well?' he says to the red parrot.

'I haven't written anything,' I say. 'I rewrote the one about the people on a bus who have pumpkins for heads.'

'Oh dear,' he says to the red parrot. 'No nuts for you.'

~

'The tradition I am writing in is very important,' I tell Erica. 'It turns things inside out.'

'No it doesn't,' says Erica.

'I mean that metaphorically,' I tell her. 'It *inverts* things.'

'What things?'

'Things that need to be inverted.'

'Like what things?'

'I don't know. Like the Sanctity of Marriage.'

'Why would *anyone* want to invert the Sanctity of Marriage?'

'To ridicule it.'

'But—'

'The Sanctity of Marriage was a bad example,' I say. 'My tradition simply gives people an alternative way of seeing things. A way they perhaps hadn't considered before.'

'No it doesn't,' says Erica. '*What* things?'

∼

I awake the next morning to find my mouth full of sand.

'Why did you pour sand into my mouth?' I ask Erica, later.

'Sand?' she says. 'Oh, yes, the sand. It was to give you an alternative way of seeing your mouth. A way you perhaps hadn't considered before.'

≈

I eat prawn sandwiches on the veranda with Steven—a security guard at the city gallery.

'Hey, there's a Man Ray exhibition just started,' he says. 'We've got twelve of his sculptures. You should come and have a look if you're out of inspiration.'

'That's great,' I say. 'I'll write a poem called "Bubble Pipe" and put *After Man Ray* under the title and the poem will begin, ' "A man smoked bubbles instead of tobacco." '

'And it could end, "What a silly, silly man he was." ' says Steven.

There is still sand in my teeth and it cracks, sickeningly, whenever I bite anything.

~

'Maybe you are being haunted by irony's ghost,' says Erica.

≈

The little red parrot has died. When I visit my patron he will not answer the door. I notice my bronze cage in a skip on the front lawn. There is a laminated notice announcing a memorial service for the parrot, yesterday.

~

A man is waiting in our living room. Erica has made pancakes and he is eating some of them. There are three squeezed segments of lemon on a plate on the table.

'He's come to arrest you,' says Erica.

The man looks at me, bashfully.

'It's not just you,' he says. 'We're arresting everyone who is suspected of flippancy.'

The handcuffs close over my wrists, as if joining me to a tradition. Before they were the handcuffs of petty vandalism and the handcuffs of sex games. Now they are handcuffs of a great institution.

'Nothing to say?' says Erica. 'You're not going to liken the handcuffs to something asinine?'

Trombone

Something tells me I'm onto something good. I've only been playing the trombone for two weeks, but already the flooded grey streets are woven with yellow ribbons and the family I don't recognise have started to smile at me with genuine warmth. Who did this, with the ribbons? I don't know. But there are fresh yellow ribbons every day. Today I stopped to buy a magazine but I threw it away because it couldn't tell me anything. Funny how the street makes you. A lodge house composes you. Someone else's problems compose you. The rattle inside a speaker defines you. The last time I carried you I saw a bird table being whisked away by a tornado. When I play my trombone, I am creating the whole street. The fake mother brings me cinnamon toast. The fake father reads the newspaper. The wallpaper is brown and decorated with tiny crests, also brown, but darker. Is this the crest of my family? It has two brown beatles and a big pair of red smiling lips arranged beneath a proscenium arch. It is a stupid crest.

The fake sister has spiky black hair and a pink leather jacket from Florence. She wears big green plastic hoop earrings. All night she stands out on the roof, a gum-chewing sentinel waiting for her boyfriend and his helicopter. The mother despairs. Patricia is only fifteen and she's already seeing a man with a helicopter.

I keep thinking I've written a song and the feeling excites me so much I forget the song and it's back to blasting out 'Summertime' again. 'Summertime', every day, every night. The father takes pride in polishing trophies with an acrid smelling salve. 'Doubtless the patterns repeat, so let's make them beautiful patterns!' is his personal motto. Etched into the wall above his head with a bread knife, it has the unnerving appearance of writing found at a grisly crime-scene.

I help the mother with the quick crossword: Don Quixote's assistant was Sancho Panza. Tiny mistakes I have made in the past persist in horrifying me—moths flicking themselves against a bulb. The brain is a bulb.

The trombone depresses me more than any other instrument—which is why I must face it, as a demon. A demon with a big, brass face. We use our faces to cope with things, sometimes holding our faces out in front of us so that whatever is coming our way hits our face first; the face is malleable and strong, like sourdough bread.

Patricia is melting a black candle onto her pink leather jacket. This is so that her boyfriend will recognise her, she tells me. There are two girls going around impersonating Patricia, same bright pink jackets, same spiky black hair and plastic green hoop earrings, because they know her boyfriend is partially sighted. One of them has already been up in his helicopter. So she's told him to feel the jacket in future for wax.

'Why black wax?' I ask her.

Only candle she had.

'And while we're on the subject,' I say, 'how does he fly the helicopter if he's partially sighted?'

He has a little assistant called Sancho Panza.

This seems like bullshit to me. Suddenly I wonder how much of what Patricia tells me is true—this is the first time I have ever doubted her. Could it be that she has always lied to me, from the very beginning? Even the nice things?

Oh, God, not the nice things. I *cleaved* to those.

Tonight, after my homework which is maths (and easy because I am not really twelve), I think I will use my family as material for a song, but the trombone refuses, preferring to write songs about clumsy policemen and crates of bananas floating down a river. I hate the trombone, but the more I practice, the more it begins to love me. It is unputdownable. The father wears flavoured cardigans—licorice and coffee flavour and, sometimes, clay.

I am trying to find the value of x when he shouts out my name and I run downstairs to find the black and white TV and my face on it. I am being disavowed as a fake little boy. The news reporter says I am really a writer pretending to be a little boy and making snide comments about the family who so generously treat me like a son. The father stares at the screen. I realise that the mother is standing behind him, clutching her mouth with a marigold glove. I run upstairs three floors and out of the fire-escape to find Patricia on the roof, her pink jacket all daubed with black wax and I ask her to let me go with her.

'What about your trombone?' she says.

'Fuck the trombone,' I say.

I can hear the scoffing of a helicopter.

Men Made of Words

a rondeaux

Men made of words live in migraine hotels
And talk not of music, but speaker cables;
Stay up to drink whisky with red lemonade,
Point out the mistakes one other has made —
Of pronunciation, directions and sales.

Some compare charts before prints of Kandinsky;
Some pick on the barmaid — Nebraskan and pretty —
Their guiding philosophy never needs telling;
The Fauvists, so colourful: what is it they're selling?
Art never hurts for the men made of words.

So if you, like I, often let down your guard
When you're drunk in the hush of a theatre courtyard;
Or, forced to find work beneath travestied arches,
You find yourself under the weight of their glances,
Make your excuse while the handshakes are hard
And run for your life from the men made of words.

Notes:

'A note on the form,' says the wolf. 'It is a *rondeaux*.'

'Yes,' I say. 'You've written "A rondeaux" underneath the title in italics.'

'You probably wouldn't understand what a rondeaux is,' says the wolf, 'because most of what you call poetry doesn't even have line breaks. This is why I am frequently asked to provide poems for current affairs, periodicals, commercial services and military organisations, whereas you are asked to provide poems solely for personal gain and the sake of your so-called career. The so-called status quo rejects traditional form on grounds that it is too traditional.'

'It seems rather mean to businessmen,' I say, 'the poem, I mean.'

'Businessmen are the diametric opposite of poetry,' says the wolf. 'Poetry is mud, businessmen are a hole.'

'It's just one of those poems where you try to make out that poets are better than ordinary people because we're more cultured and sensitive,'

I complain, opening a rocket lolly.

'It may not be true in your case,' says the wolf, 'but then you are part of the academic machine: you write favourable reviews of your friends so they shortlist you for things and vice versa. And nobody buys your books. Maybe you should try using a rhyme scheme once in a while, that's all I'm saying. Ooh, rocket lollies! Can I have one?'

'This is the last.'

from Sexual Fantasies Of The Inuit Warriors

'. . . campfire stories, essentially, the aim of the contest was to achieve some form of sexual arousal by the most circuitous route possible—sort of a tantric dirty limerick. One warrior must speak until the tallow candle burns down, at which point a new one is lit and the story is passed to the next . . .'

I.

In this fantasy I am represented by three killer whales, bright blue, yellow and red like illustrations from a cheap children's book. The whales swim together, their paths weaving in and out, each taking their turn as the leader. However far they stray from one another, they are still connected because they are all *me*. When the bright red killer whale is in the lead I become aware of a cruise liner in the water above us and my vision tracks upwards as quickly as a bubble rising through a glass. I am still the three whales, but now I am also sitting in the cruise ship's restaurant, opposite a beautiful 26 year old woman (she has a badge reading 26 TODAY!) who has long auburn hair and bottle-green eyes. When she stoops to pick up the corkscrew I am unable to resist looking down her blouse, wherein I see a drawing-room farce that is too aware of the conventions of the genre and keeps undercutting the gags with self-conscious stuttering and metafictional asides. At first this was charming, but now, three acts in, the raised eyebrows are becoming unbearable. Also, I am struggling to keep the three whales swimming in some kind of synchronicity—at least they should all be *visible* to one another —and making conversation with the beautiful woman about her Masters degree in theatre praxis. All at once, the waiter arrives with a silver tray of way too many champagne glasses; the red whale sings in horror, turns on its tail and begins swimming, fast, in the opposite direction; the bright yellow whale is harpooned and I stand up, suddenly, knocking over the table. I put out my hand to steady myself, but my arm launches into the tray of champagne flutes and they fall to the ground like a cathedral being demolished for no good reason. Back in her room I am drinking a glass of cough medicine and she is sitting on the bed singing a sad song about three whales. She unfastens her stays to reveal a darkly comic naturalistic drama about family life and psychopathology. It is not a bad play, but the dialogue is sometimes overly expositional.

II.

A branch taps at the rain-lashed porthole—which doesn't strike me as odd until I remember we have been at sea for five days. When I go to the window I see that we have run aground in the middle of a Cubist mansion. Which is to say, whatever it was before, it is now Cubist, having been smashed by a boat. Our *en suite* has been ripped off and a rift leads directly onto a stone spiral-staircase which leads upwards. Or downwards. I take my partner's hand and we climb the stairs into a great dining hall, a figure dressed in purple velvet stands with his back to us. When the figure in the purple cloak turns around I notice that he has a big, flat, smooth, slate-blue face and a long, cavernous mouth. He is King of the Whales and he is singing 'What do You Get When You Fall in Love?' in a shameless baritone. I ask my partner with the auburn hair what her name is so that I can introduce her, but when she says,

'Cecily,'

the word swells to the size of a double-decker bus and I find myself running, at knee-jarring speed, down the inside camber of a capital letter 'C'. When I reach the lip I jump off and haul myself up the black, rubbery side of a lower case 'e', from whence it is only a short leap to the little mahogany 'c', the roof of which bends unpleasantly under my feet, making the sloping pivot of the 'i' difficult to reach. I jump, hands out before me, but hopelessly miss and fall through the space between the two letters, landing on a thoroughly ordinary 'of', the size of which is so small and unremarkable I can almost hear a human voice saying it—and then I am standing in the Cubist dining hall again, one hand on the offending passage of my autobiography, one hand gripping C's arm as she says, '. . . of course, it is very dangerous for me to say it.'

III.

Women with parasols and men with thick waxy moustaches are trouping out of the jack-knifed cruise liner like ants from a foot-long club sandwich. They pass us and walk down the spiral staircase and I wonder if perhaps I could learn something from their easy adaptation to the new circumstances. The King of Whales nods at each one of them in solidarity—his life has changed for the worse, too. The ship's captain has put on a blood-red suit as a symbol of apology. C. and I follow the ladies and gentlemen down the spiral staircase, but are distracted by the smell of flowers coming from a dark doorway. A funeral? Already? We pass through the heavy curtain and take a seat in a white prefabricated room full of tables and students. It is a 'life-coaching' seminar. On the whiteboard at the moment are two statements: 'The way you get on with others' and 'The decisions you make', both of which, I assume, are being taught as important things for the students to consider. We are told to visualise our lives as a row of terraced houses, one house to represent each year. I look across at C. and she is dissolving in tears. Within moments she is no more than a pile of bubbles on the new grey carpet. 'Why not try ringing one of the doorbells?' suggests the instructor. 'Maybe the door you are standing outside has no doorbell. What is the number on this door? 26? 14? Is the number cut out of brass or written on a scrap of paper and taped to the door? Why not try knocking on the door?' My clothes feel tight under my armpits. I look down to find I am wearing a navy blue postman's uniform. There is a package in my hands addressed to number 16. The houses are tall Georgian red-bricks. I walk down the terraced street until I reach number 16. I ring the doorbell . . .

Spade

Flat-faced clown of the gazebo,
Lever that punctures the world,
A see-saw we cleave to and see our fate
Rising on the other side.
Piano of the shed's orchestra,
A stick fastened to an evil
cast-iron cartoon seagull.
The opposite of a knife:
You cannot be used accidentally.
The force and stance required
Renders us one animal.
When the earth is gravelly
We sound like a distant car starting.
When muddy, satisfying as a new word
Used surreptitiously in the right context.
Once the hole is dug the only thing
I cannot bury in it is you;
Tamping down the sewn earth
Like gunpowder in a canon.
Puppet on a blue-screen,
Dancing like a smug wand,
Suddenly disembodied,
From me, your erstwhile fossor,
Your mortal, flubby ballast,
Your spluttering engine.

Gravedigger: *The Movie*

I found my spirit of defiance in an old wooden chest labelled 'Traditions'. It had a note attached to it reading,

Hope you make better use of this than I did. Mum x x

In my culture young women must live with a gravedigger between the ages of 8 and 16 — to give them a profound sense of mortality. I hated my gravedigger so thoroughly that as soon as I was of age, I re-married and left him digging graves in the paddock under a black sunset. I was happy, as if I had lived in a woodcut for 8 years and now lived in a little girl's crayon drawing of a house. My husband had a smooth, formless texture and said he would bite anyone who upset me. A kettle hung over the fireplace — although both the kettle and the fireplace were electric. A retired astronaut lived in a cottage at the end of a peach grove to the North West of me — exactly the direction I happen to be facing now. The thought of meeting another new person was like shaking crumbs of gold out of the silt so starved of company had I been until now. Some days it rained thick black oil over everything, but if I buried my face in my hands the oil vanished and the colours returned.

A glitch in the corner of my eye warned me that the scene was about to end.

~

You *let* a thousand flowers bloom by not stamping on them — and this implies no studious work on your part, nor even any great act of restraint. I read essays all day, sitting in a swing — and when the voices became disagreeable to me I dropped the periodical and swung all the higher. Too many journalists are like too many biscuits. 'If you are proud of your nationality, be proud of the worst things about it. Slap children to make sure they are still alive. These are not tender times. Clean the ashes off the toys you found among the debris and give them to your dogs to chew,' said one. '*Webster's* defines a civilian as "an accident waiting to happen."' Well, I could agree with that. I found something to cherish in their opinions. I got behind them like an orderly queue. They seemed to bring something out of my guilt and frustration the way a landscape artist brings something out of a landscape. 'In this essay I will be discussing, etc.'

~

I had forgotten what it was to be hungry and meaning blossomed everywhere. My new husband suggested we visit the gravedigger to show there were no hard feelings. He was given to kind but misguided gestures, my husband. For instance, yesterday he had taken baskets of peaches to the retired astronaut. 'What the hell am I supposed to do with these?' barked the astronaut. 'I *live* in a godamn peach grove.' When my husband pointed out that peaches looked like Jupiter he was asked impolitely to leave. I had no doubt visiting my gravedigger would be just as pointless. As we approached his shack I could feel interminable train delays and hospital visits building up in my stomach. The gravedigger had put up a sign: 'PATRONS ARE KINDLY ASKED TO CLAP ALONG WITH MY UNCONTAINABLE WEEPING'. I affected the expression of an overworked civil servant, my husband the expression of an adolescent left in charge of an ornamental fossil shop, and we rang my gravedigger's doorbell. He appeared, rubbing his eyes and told us to beat it.

~

I was such a good listener I would just sit there on the windowsill sometimes, listening. The empty rooms I left behind me would fill with laughing children, trapped in amber—I mean rooms in demolished houses, the solid ones. My husband was so busy at the paint factory all day I started to visit the retired astronaut. I listened to him and offered him my body when I wasn't using it; it was the time of the sexual revolution. The monsters I saw when I closed my eyes were emerging from a rift in the sky. He described me as good, but not as good as space travel. I said, 'Well, that's what you get for seeing your planet at a distance,' and left him staring at the peach trees.

～

Now I lived in a series of limited edition prints—rejected from the final run because the colours bled at the edges or had been badly transposed. A week passed without new adventures. My husband became cold and malleable—always arriving home from somewhere with a buttoned-up coat and an unconvincing story. As it transpired, he had been made Unconvincing Story editor for a new local sitcom to be screened in the Autumn. 'You're going to love it,' he told me. 'I've based one of the characters on you—you know, the crazy things you say.' The unconvincing stories were parallelogram in shape and small and dark grey. They unfolded awkwardly and with only one other colour sometimes —a deep maroon. His reticence only solidified my affair with the retired astronaut: I kissed him for longer, held him tighter, knocked insistently on the top of his head.

～

It looked like my biography was a technical description of a medicine, given away with the box, the key events side-effects. How, by Jupiter, do you kill a man with a peach? I assume he first has to agree to the terms. Anyway, it was neat. I lived in a single frame, one of twenty-five in a second of footage—my husband murdered the retired astronaut by shoving a parasol down his throat—which would have been funny if this were a cartoon— and although the brevity astonished me, I was so thankful. He dressed the corpse in a space-suit he found in the wardrobe and dragged it to my gravedigger's house—which was oilier and darker than ever, covered in a contingency of crows and their parasites. My gravedigger looked out of his window and soon appeared in the woodchips with a shovel which he used, in the first instance, to stave in my husband's head like it was a bad automatic piano and, in the second instance, to dig his (my husband's) and the astronaut's graves. His letter of apology was ruined by the typographical representation of conceited laughter and the right margin, in certain lights, resembled his cackling face in profile. I assumed he would take me back—as was the tradition. Everything melted around the edges and the film stock snickered on its reel. At dawn I took off for the railway station with a basket of peaches and a book of ruined photographs. 'Now for a word from our sponsors,' I said, frothily.